unpacking

unpacking

Noelle Rousseau

and He said to me
write

for the broken and the lost
for those who need to be seen
and for those who feel alone

write

for the abused
the misunderstood
and for those who carry more than they should

so i did

for those that made me believe in love again

but mostly, for hannah, beth and kev

contents:

lost.. page 10

searching...page 81

healing..page 98

home...page 149

lost

to tell the story
of an overcomer
you must first
tell the story
of the things
that overcame them

the promise of fall sends a chill
through my bones
and the air is heavy with grief
anger and hostility have become the backbone
for every interaction
i can't stand it

we are all so incredibly lost and alone

———————————

i should be happy, but i'm not. most days i struggle to keep my head above the waves and the solitude of sadness seems to envelope me.

i think maybe misery has become my home. a safe place with no chains to which i keep returning despite the gnawing and yearning for so much more

i want to be happy, but i'm not. i've tried meditating and writing and screaming away this emptiness that seems to hang in my chest like dirty laundry

i have nothing to say that rivals the silence
and i can't seem to try anymore

———————————

i need to be happy, but the journey there seems so long, and the more i return to this place of desolation the harder it gets to leave

the pain asks nothing from me but to feel

i should be happy, but i'm not, and i think the hardest thing to admit is that i really don't mind being lazy and blind to the life i could have if i stopped seeing safety in sadness

"the sky is on fire"
she said

"and although it is terribly grim,
i wish i was too"

"burn me alive, at least i'll feel something"

the worst part is
people will set you on fire
with their words
and pour apathy out
like it's water

no one warned us that by twenty-five
most of us would be searching for death
instead of searching for soulmates

no one warned us that by twenty-five
we'd be so sick of surviving we could
barely go on living in a world that puts its
weight on our backs

and asks us why we're breaking

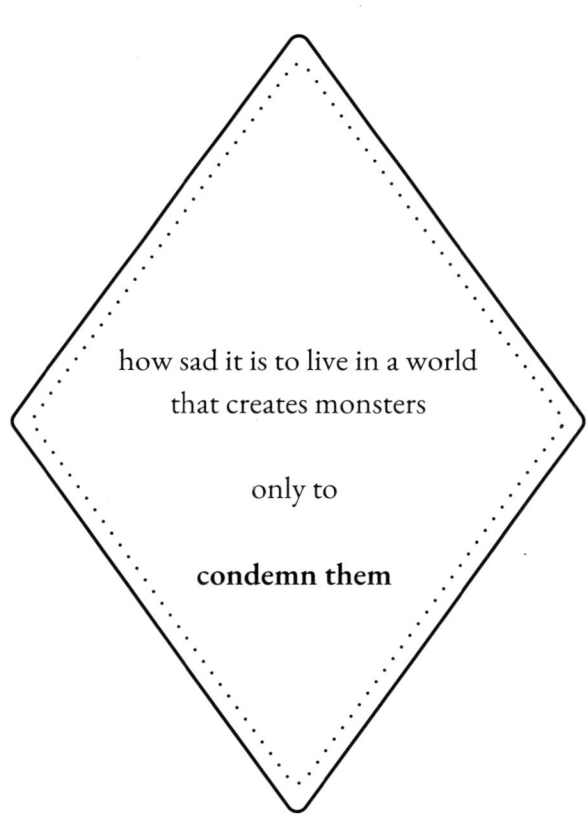

how sad it is to live in a world
that creates monsters

only to

condemn them

growing up, kids bullied me
because i wasn't enough

now,
adults bully me
for being
too
much

the world asks me to change
does it not understand?

i have not yet figured out who I am

misery

i've spent years trying to be understood
by those that lacked such abilities

i was silenced by so many people
i didn't notice when i
started silencing
myself

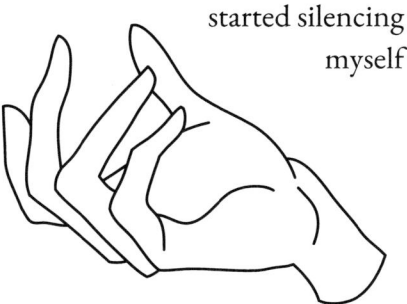

it's my assumptions
that keep me
captive

- i am a prisoner of the past

i hate it here
in this endless labyrinth of expectations
and impossible standards
stuck running until my legs become weak
only to end up further behind

i

      am

         drowing

trying to save face
my mind is a prison i cannot escape

. - i wish i didn't care what they think

the first time a boy kissed me
i learned what fear felt like

i was nine

less than ten years old when i was first told
the most sinister lie
my body is not my own

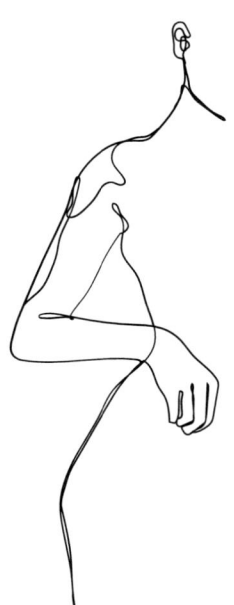

all these years spent
dressing to get noticed
and instead i got
assaulted

- i wish i was invisible

when i was 16, and down on my knees for the first time i wasn't thinking about 23

i wasn't thinking about the misery and pain that came from giving to men again and again, i was young, probably dumb for ignoring what everyone says,

"don't give it up
he'll think you're a slut
just keep your mouth shut and be sensible"

when i was 18 and in love for the first time i wasn't thinking about 23.

i didn't realize i was teaching myself to be spineless by saying yes based on promises that would never be kept, that giving in and giving up would become my go to

maybe, i would have done different
if i was thinking about you

when i was 21 and heartbroken for the first time i wasn't thinking about how i was going to say no. i was too busy saying yes to nights spent undressed, wrapped in the silence of 2am and convinced nothing mattered

giving it up again and again because somehow by 21 i learned what had to be done to avoid the pain and the shame of saying no

somehow by 21 i learned that 'no 'really didn't have an effect on a boy that wants sex, so by 23, when i didn't say yes but i didn't know how to say no when he finally got me alone

it broke me

when i was 16, i wasn't thinking about 23
when "my choice"suddenly became his

- lessons

"and tell me," he asked

"where is the line,
 between sacrifice and self-destruction?"

- i only know how to give

every day i look in the mirror and hate myself into submission

i feel so undeserving

maybe that's why i'm settling

i think i hated myself so loudly
i taught them to hate me
too

the first love, was like a fairytale
without the happy ending

he was using me to be
all he could not

"you do not love me," i say

"you barely know me"

your silence draws the words from my mouth

"you love the you you see in me"

its three o'clock in the morning and all i can think
about is how you didn't ask for a map of the galaxies
in my head

you never asked if my mother was soft and kind or
why my knuckles go white from gripping car doors on
left hand turns

or why i always feel so incredibly behind

you never gave curiosity to my obsession with the sky
and never asked where i hoped i would land in a year

or five

you never asked me who i was, your childish desires
satisfied only with the way i was wrapped

you stopped at the cover
and didn't read the book

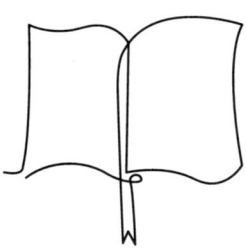

"perfect"
the poisoned word tumbled
from your sweet honey lips

and i reminisced on how long
i had craved perfection
and dreamed of being flawless
my body starving for it
my skin bleeding for it

"perfect"
you called me
the words like a knife slicing my soul into pieces

i ached for you to see how painfully wrong you were
to show you my scars
and give voices to the demons in my head

but i searched for explanations
and found silence instead

you saw me as an illusion

a flower growing in the midst of a burning forest
and i wished you were right

but i have always been destruction
the flames of the fire

and if you saw that, you'd leave

- flowers grow, fire burns

the second love will give you hope

but hope is a flimsy foundation

"what are you afraid of?"

his voice taunts me

"that this one will be just like the last"

you are a second chance
an elixir for the agony of a twice broken heart
you are a thunderstorm in august

sudden
unexpected
powerful

and you are the feeling after the rain
the cold fresh air and the sound of the birds
their beautiful melody in every word you speak

you are confusion and frustration
chased with hope to cut the sting

you are regret and contentedness intertwined into a
melancholy symphony to which there is no conductor

you are friday nights at 12 o'clock
ten minute drives and kissing goodbye

you are a book of lovely thoughts
with a brutally tragic ending
a peaceful comfort and a ticking clock

and I am biding my time

- i know how this ends

he called forth discomfort in me, shaky hands and weak knees. how flawlessly he wore the juxtaposition of heaven and hell on his sleeve; heart divided across the dimensions

his gaze tore through me, leaving my soul exposed and my walls near crumbling. i knew in an instant that my worst nightmare and my safe haven shared the same stormy eyes and soothing smokey voice

between the continuous noise of the fan in his patio door and the train outside, i could hear the rhythm in his chest

my fingers ran slowly down his sternum tangling in his dark hair. my eyes were heavy and my thoughts intertwined with the smell of his cologne.

lying there in the clouds of the midnight sun
i wondered if forever smelled like tuscan leather
and the whiskey on his lips

- intoxicated

i am terrified of you and i, love
and this unknown place we exist
that has dissolved the illusion of safety
i once felt in isolation

i am terrified of all i am,
and more so of all i am not
suspended between the agony i perceive
that comes with giving in and feeling
and the simplicity of seclusion

you are an unknown language
feelings that do not translate to paper
yet i keep trying
wringing my heart out
and arranging spilled blood into words
in attempts to make sense of the way you
unravel me,
love

i am a prisoner of the in-between
wanting to give in
but part of me convinced
you're lying

i thought about setting my thoughts free
letting words held captive
escape between my teeth

but my tongue was tied in knots

despite writing a novel of feelings titled for you

saying 'i love you'
gave you just too much power

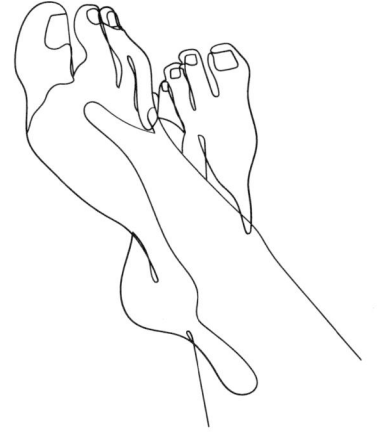

i exist
with him
one foot in and
one foot
out

how well i wear the contradiction
of far too much
and never enough

it's 10pm and you'll stumble over your words
and omit what stings of honesty. his hand will
brush your arm and you'll wait in anticipation
to feel electricity like the first time your lips
met on the roof of his car in the chilled spring
air; but instead, you recoil.

sweaty palms replace butterflies and your heart
will feel empty and cold in your chest despite
the warmth of his skin.
caution; you'll call it, as you tremble with fear.

his eyes are full of galaxies and you almost fall
victim to the sweetness of honey oozing from
his lips; but when he says 'i love you' you'll
wonder why reciprocation is a noose not a
milestone.

- caution

there was a bittersweet taste to our almost love
once a clear picture

simple

now a smokey haze of sloppy judgment
and unsaid words
fuelled by 3 a.m. and the honey on your lips

missing definitions and elaborate ambiguity
holding hostage what *could* be

- the words you never say

i don't want the warmth of a body
who's eyes have never held my gaze
for long enough to see my soul
i don't want the breath
of lips that have not whispered my name
as if it was a life and a home wrapped
into one
i don't want the silence of breathing
or the screaming of unsaid words
questions, or expectations

i want the familiarity of a heartbeat
and the warmth of a smile
that despite everything
hold the promise
of forever

- i want a non-fiction love

when it is 2 am and i cannot sleep
i hope it means
you are thinking of me

perhaps it's foolish to assume that your essence
has the power
to travel across the ocean, stirring my mind
and wrapping me in an empty longing

but if i am wake
as the world sleeps peacefully outside
the only worthwhile cause i have ever known
is you

i painted so many pictures of you in my head
hoping you would stay pure
and that your words would always radiate warmth
in the coldest corners of my heart

such a pity that you chose to engulf me completely
instead
and leave ashes where my life once was

someday is a cruel tease
void of the finite reality of goodbye
but soaked in false hope and heartbreak

we could not dwell there forever
in the arms of possibility

but
i'll always love that picture of you i painted
of what you could have been

unspoken words bled from the same fingertips
that once tangled in your hair

i am spilling all my secrets onto paper
the ones that were meant for your ears

the atmosphere changed as time stood still, the noise of
the water pouring from the bathtub faucet fell on my
ears like a lullaby, blocking out the hum of traffic
outside my frosted window

the water was running out of room, grazing my jawline
now

i thought about you briefly, how you used to slide in
behind me and wrap your arms around my tired body,
drowning out reality

i wanted to drown in oceans of love. the kind that makes
your soul giggle and lights the night sky on fire. i wanted
two a.m. drunk kisses and sunday morning coffee in bed
staring at the golden flecks in your sapphire eyes
i wanted to jump off the cliff
to dive off the deep end and love you without caution

you wanted to dip your toes in my rivers
and stay in quiet waters

you wanted a shallow love

the realization hit as the water rose above my head
the world silently fading as i drowned
in the aftermath
of loving you more than you could ever return

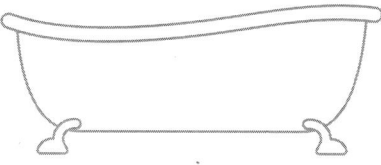

my hands traced from my lips to my neck
winding over my collarbone
sliding over each rib
down my sternum

stopping
in hesitation
at my hips

how strange to touch a body
wishing your hands on it instead

that was always the most worrisome part
how utterly ruined i was
by only the concept
of you

you made pathetic maybe's
and ambiguous forevers
sound melodic
and assuring

like your voice was a warm summer breeze
or the late august sun on my cheek
but the seasons changed
and your words grew cold
and the space between what i needed
and what you had to offer
became two hands to my throat

"i told you, i warned you"

i knew you were right

i gladly wore your hands as a noose

i am distressed, love
left standing in this wreckage

in all your glory you were only ever the chaos
i so viciously fought off

you were never a safe place
just intimidating and exciting
and *oh*
the thrill of you never compared to the emptiness
of the aftermath

as i breathed you in one last time
and felt your poison fill my lungs
my image of you grew blurry

that was it
the moment i knew
every last part of me was

entirely
      consumed

"i guess that's the catch"

my voice trembled

"we never spoke the same language, you and i"

an icy blue tear falls from my sad eyes

"i spoke the language of promises and reality, and you wrote a fairytale on my skin with your lips"

he was silent, his silhouette slowly slumping from the bed

"you knew this was the book we were writing"

he was right

temporary was always the title to our story

<u>one</u>

we sat across from each other in a diner at 9am. i was hungover and 10 minutes late. he told me about his mother's cooking and we ate pancakes.

<u>two</u>

he opened the car door for me and got a parking ticket while we ate dinner. my stomach was in knots from the atrocious amount of food we ate, and when he kissed me on his couch later that night i imagined what his skin might feel like on mine.

<u>three</u>

the restaurant was dark and the food was subpar. i have never laughed as hard as i did sitting on the floor of his apartment at 10pm talking about dancing cars and upside down houses.

<u>four</u>

he kissed me again, but this time was different. he kissed me with desperation; like it was the first time and the last time and the only time. he kissed me, and i got lost. i did not know where he ended and i began. he kissed me and i forgot my name and i forgot that my head hurt and i forgot that i was scared of him.

<u>five</u>
my car was parked far away and the morning air was cold. he kissed me goodbye and said "i'll see you soon". i saw him look back as i drove away, my shaking hands fumbling with a cigarette as i wiped the sleep from my eyes.

<u>six</u>
i sped home. i wanted to rinse my skin of him and run away from the obligations of 'soon'. i wanted to forget the way he touched me and the scent of his cologne.

<u>seven</u>
i sat in the shower until my skin was wrinkled and the water was cold. i wondered when i'd stop running from anyone that didn't feel like you.

when i was a little girl i made bets on raindrops
as our worn out van sat parked and the sky collapsed
i watched, mesmerized

two drops racing down the window
and i guessed which one would wind the easiest path
disappearing from the pane to the pavement

funny, no matter which one beat the other
i held to my choice

the sky cried
for it knew
i'd hold to you too

loneliness clings to my bones
as the taste of his lips vanishes
the warmth of his body replaced
by cold sheets and a deafening silence

i've been drowning in indifference
flirting with fleeting pleasure
and building a fortress out of moments
that were never meant to last

i don't know how to let you go
i don't know how to move forward

but i can't keep sitting here pretending
like some day you'll change

love doesn't work like that

i guess it's time to face the truth

i can't keep kissing strangers
and pretending that they're you

- make believe

the third love starts with questions

"why does love always feel like war?"

and it finishes with answers:

"you have never known love before"

and there you came
a sword for a tongue
and death in your eyes
you were destined
always
to be my demise

love is patient, love is kind
so tell me
why does it feel like i'm losing my mind?

every day the air gets thicker
and i feel more like a sinner
every time he reminds me of all the men i left behind

every word he says makes me feel dirty
hanging from my pale white skin like thick black tar

i'm still trying to understand how he can label me a
whore
and get angry when i say no
like he's somehow above it

i think maybe he loves it when i cry

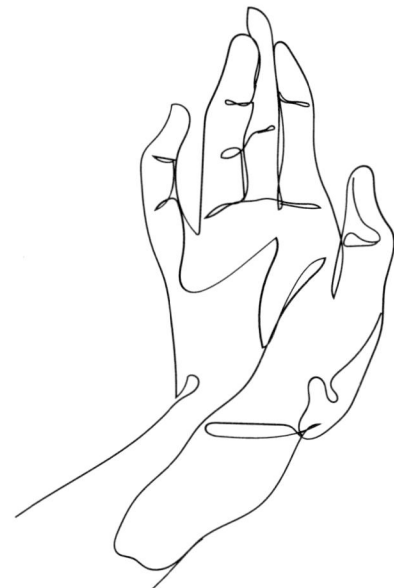

his words hurt
more
than i imagined
his hands would

- some days i wish he hit me instead

when i asked you what we were doing here
pretending to love each other
you didn't have an answer

and somehow that was my fault

- blame

you held me hostage
with the secrets
i told you

no wonder i blamed myself

you made me look insane
as if you weren't the one who drove me there

how easy it was
to fall victim to lies
so carefully disguised
as the truth

i remember that night standing on my balcony
your eyes caught the sun
as you spun your web of lies

and that's the sad part

i thought you were the one

and that love would conquer all

and now i don't know what i hate more:

the fact that you deceived me
or the fact that i believed

you made chaos into art
as i came unraveled in your arms
"love" you called it
with each scar to my heart
but love was never meant to hurt

this year, i met heartbreak and welcomed grief into my home. i learned that life is cruel and uncalled for and nothing but chaos the majority of the time. i learned that the sun will rise and set and that the days will go by whether you're there to see them or not

i learned that the future is an illusion and the past is a prison, and in learning to let go i learned to hold on to what mattered

this year i learned that people will betray you, and justify it. they will cross every line you draw with their pride by their side and let their opinions tie a noose around your neck. i learned that not everyone is good, and that some people are evil

this year taught me strength, it taught me sadness and how to handle the restlessness of existing in the in-between

and the most important lesson: we think we have time *but time is fleeting*

grief
i think
is an awakening of sorts

an awakening to all the things
you took for granted
all the things you lack
and all the ways you'll have to grow
in their absence

- *when i lost you i lost me too*

i've felt a little stuck since you left
the rest of the world is going about their business
and God as my witness

i can't

every time i feel like i am ready to stop existing in
this silent space of safety
where i act like life is a mystery
i seem to end up staying put

it's easier than pretending every step forward isn't
a step without you

it's more simple than telling myself some bullshit
story about you being there with me in spirit

and pretending like knowing you'll never be there
to walk me down the aisle
or hold my child in your arms
isn't
killing me

the world feels empty since you left
empty of laughter and hope
of possibility
empty of dreams

i used to look around and see memories
but with every day that passes things grow blurry
and i wonder if someday the space you occupied
in my mind will be too buried to find

i'm scared that i didn't write enough down

but how do you put a soul on paper?

how are you supposed to capture a larger than life
impact in a few meager words?

how do you write about a life so full of love when
all you see is the space it no longer holds

how do you move forward *when it feels so much
like moving on?*

                              - unanswered questions

heaven feels far away today
i keep finding pieces of you in everyone i meet
and it feels like grief is really just insanity that hits
closer to home

God
i feel so alone down here

tonight i realized that i don't remember what it felt like to hug you. i don't remember what it smelled like when i buried my face in your chest on my bad days and when i really let that sink in, **everything goes blank**

trying to write about grief is like trying to count the number of times i'll sit down at a table that should have one more setting, or the number of holidays i'll have to focus on just getting though, *it's never ending*

trying to write about grief is like trying to ignore the vastness of this void i'm supposed to call "life"

sure, some days i'm okay, but lately i'm searching for you everywhere in everyone i meet and i don't know how to write about this miserable empty place inside my heart i can't escape because you're never coming back and the memories are fading

and i am frozen in time
just trying to figure out how to miss you without breaking
and failing

i feel the grief in the morning when the first rays of sun
break past the horizon
i still remember the 5 a.m. wake ups to go capture the
sunrise with you

i feel the warmth of the sun mixed with the memory of
your smile
every summer day spent outside riding bikes

and sometimes i still get angry at the kids without
helmets
but deep down i can't help but feel peace
because helmet
or not
i know it was your time

i wish you could see the world since you left
it's falling apart at the seams and it's funny some days, i
feel i am too

i'm trying to be strong but everything's wrong
and i miss you

- acceptance feels like sadness

i wondered if the rise and fall of my chest was
meant to feel so laboured
it felt like second nature to struggle
breathing in the black smoke of tobacco
and ferociously exhaling the breath i was holding

waiting
in suspense

hoping to feel different

but as my lungs became tired and my bones ached
under the weight of my bittersweet existence
i knew
these were burdens picked just for me

so as i had done
so many times before
i etched the lessons on my skin
and supported my weight on their wisdom

one step at a time

on i go

please,
remember every night you spent submerged in the
lukewarm water of a bath you ran two hours ago
salty black tears painting the pain on your skin
reminding you that despite desperate attempts to
dissociate and the bottle in your hand
you can never escape how you feel

remember how you broke beneath the weight of things
that were never yours to carry
remember the blood on your wrists and the nights you
spent in strangers beds trying to feel alive
but mostly
remember
that you survived
that despite your heavy chest and the darkness you held
inside, you still saw value in being alive

- the good parts of pain

searching

part of me was always searching
for people i had never met
places i had never been
and love i had never felt

- i've been looking for myself

maybe that
was where it started
with this poisonous belief
that i had to be less
to be loved

<u>loopholes</u>

if i blame myself
you lose your power

i was always so good at making excuses
for everyone but me

so good at ignoring the places
boundaries should exist
as if somehow it would make me strong

but instead, *it made me weak*

<u>roadblocks</u>

i had always been the only thing
standing in my way

do you stay because it's love
or do you stay
because
it's
easy?

it has taken me my whole life
until this point
to understand

being alone does not equate
to being lonely
it is no one's responsibility
to fulfill me

i think we all want to know
that our hurt is worth something
in the end

so we beg for sympathy
instead of respect

i may have understood
but that does not mean
i should have
stayed

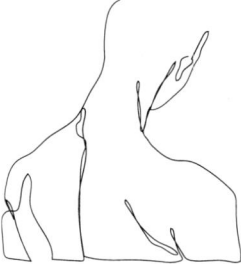

you said i could talk about anything
and then buried me alive
when i did

the most important promises
i have ever made
were to myself

yet those were the ones
most easily broken

- *let down*

i've come to know this to be true,
we project what we cannot accept

i'm sorry for the times i hated me
by hating you

when caring became painful
i chose indifference
and wondered why i felt so numb

- *lukewarm*

the in-between is a cruel place
that promises two choices
and leaves you with

none

i think i was always waiting
for someone
to tell me
they loved chaos
so i wouldn't need
to explain myself

maybe that is the answer
i was always trying to find

how i could expect to see God's plan
when i was busy telling him mine?

healing

i remember the feeling
my freshly polished nails
clawing
at the emptiness in my chest
i wondered how it would feel if they tore a hole so big it
consumed me
drowning my pain in the blackness
and i
following
into the abyss

but instead, your hand reached in
and held my heart in your flaming palm
and i knew
right then
my soul engulfed in your inferno
that if depths like this existed,
heaven must too

and there
in the fire
you brought a faithless woman
to her knees

it grew inside of me like an old oak
with its roots tangled up in my guts
and its vines around my bones
until it was me
and my lungs were failing in the claustrophobia
as i frantically tried to find the place
where it attached itself to me

my cold, boney fingers clawing through my skin
ripping back the layers in desperation

and i bled
and i bled
my insides exposed

colour drained from my cheeks as
truth cascaded from my wounds

there was nothing to rip out
no demons inside

it was only me
all along

i fought until my body shook
writhing in the pain of the breaking
of all that i am
no
all that i was

i fought with a soul that was week
until my knees fell at his feet
and that
is where it began
the healing

breathing is a small rebellion
that says

"i am alive, despite it all"

when you begin again for the hundredth time

when you pull your aching bones
from the cold hard floor

 remember, if you can
the times you have before

then stand
again

and bravely fight the war

it was in the realizing
that it had to start with someone
that i determined:
it should start

       with

          me

forgiveness is taking the gun they pointed
at you

and disarming it
not using it

we were never meant to hurt others
the way they hurt us

the abuse didn't start with me

**but it ends
with
me**

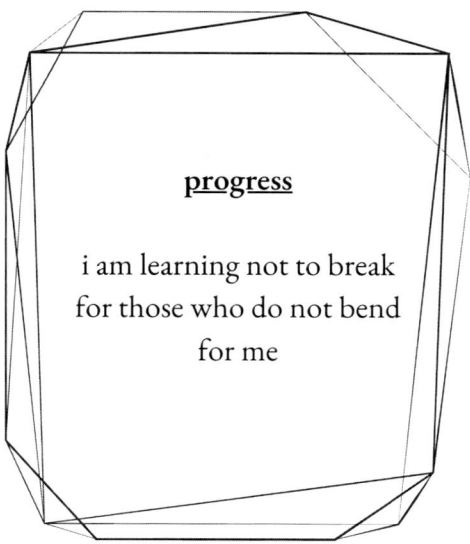

<u>progress</u>

i am learning not to break
for those who do not bend
for me

if someone does not understand you
 it is
    not
       your job

to become
less
complex

you silence the voices that beg you to be more
by simply asking
how?
i cannot be more than i am

- they don't see the ways you're growing

"i have no respect"

they say with their hands to our necks
because somehow now it's normal
to mistreat those we don't agree with
the people we've deemed ignorant
not even giving them a chance to explain
telling them it's all in vain
 because
 their belief
 is invalid

"they don't deserve empathy"
they preach in the streets as we struggle

i wish they knew what it was like, being told you're
worth less because of one decision
when they don't even know the reason you made it

"choices have consequences" they scream
as an excuse to not acknowledge our pain

as if somehow being kind
would put a mark on their name
so incapable of caring they simply look away
and focus their gaze somewhere else

"i care about them" they say

"they made the right choice"

as if selective sympathy is something to brag about

i'm tired of explaining
i'm tired of complaining
but love is not love when it's conditional

love is not love if not put into practice
with patience and kindness

and love is not love when that love wants control

- you get your choice, i get mine

somewhere along the line,
 we lost sight of love

somewhere between the arms of parents
so conditioned by the world we live in
and the desire for a fairytale
we replaced patience with passion
and kindness with coincidence

settling for less than we deserve
so afraid of missing out
if we laid it all out
and said

 "that is not love, it's control"

and instead of begging for respect we begged for sex
ending up in strangers beds looking for connection
thinking we were the exception

that love was meant to be messy, but it's not.

somewhere along the line we forgot
that love is not passion or lust or control
it is not painful despite what we're told
but it's hard

real love requires vulnerability
its not asking "what can you give me"
but slowly falling into a dance of give and take

 its trust
its loyalty
and it does not ask you to change

real love is unconditional
accepting

it says i see you
and doesn't hide away or shy away
from things we think are flaws

real love is not words
and it is not temporary

sometime ago we forgot
that love is a choice
and it's one we must make every day

- it takes work

i think the reason i had so much trouble admitting he
manipulated me
i think why it was so impossible to be vulnerable
about the pain he inflicted
and all the ways he made me bleed
 was because i didn't want to be seen
 as weak

i didn't want to be seen as stupid or naive
i didn't want to believe that i could be tricked
that i had blind spots that made me forget every time
he mustered a feeble apology
every time he lied and said "sorry"

i didn't want to be a woman that had to be afraid of
the next guy i meet online that makes me feel safe
and turns out to be faking it when he tells me i can
trust him
so i tell him i love him
 enough times that i believe it too

i don't want to spend my life unlearning how to love
these narcissistic men
that play games with my head

i don't want to fall apart every time i admit
all these things i think may be better unsaid

i am enough
and enough is enough

- i didn't deserve it
(and neither do you)

tell me, why did i have to work so hard
to earn the respect of those
who didn't care about earning mine?

i sat with my sadness today
and instead of trying to define it
instead of letting it consume my identity
i just
felt it
and let it be what it was
a cut that would heal much quicker
if i didn't make it more than it was

when grief has crushed your soul
and left a hole in place of your heart

cling to joy
fight the darkness

one second
one minute
one day at a time

rebel against that which tries to hold you back

despite what he says, you are not crazy

you are not stupid or worthless and
oh my God
you are not wrong to demand respect

you are not needy
for expecting love to be shown to you

despite what he says, you do deserve better
i promise you it's out there
girl stop giving to a man who keeps taking
who attacks your self worth
and makes you feel helpless

because you are not helpless

you are resilient and worthy
and capable of setting the world on fire
with your spark

despite what he says

you are enough

you made the best decision you could
at the time
you cannot beat yourself up
for missing the signs
because if you knew better

you would have done better

- relief

it wasn't love
if i could tell my younger self three words
i'd scream those ones so loud
it drowned everything out

it wasn't love
it was always too much or simply never enough
a vicious cycle of incredible highs
and soul crushing lows
meant to leave you feeling helpless
so you'd think less about the pain
and more about how you could change

it wasn't love
he just wanted the control he couldn't get over himself
so obsessed with your flaws
he looked right past his own
he didn't come to save you

you came to save yourself

i do not regret the love
i gave to you
because love is not
limited in supply

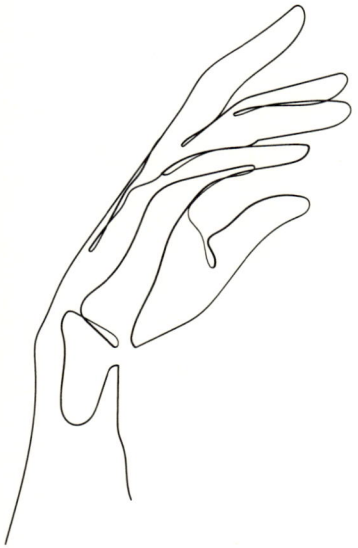

but mostly i love knowing that if we meet again sometime down the road we will be strangers

you'll look at me and expect to see the girl you tried to break barely hanging on, but you won't find me sticking around in the hell you put me through

no
 i'll be long gone

if we meet again someday you'll see a face with wrinkles from smiling at everything i've found joy in since you. you'll see a girl that rebuilt a life that is even better than the one she had before, and i hope you know,

i don't care if you care

because the best part is if we ever meet again you will realize what you lost and it will already be gone. you see i have moved on, i have healed, i have grown

so if we ever meet again, we will be strangers because the girl you tried to destroy is no more

someone better has taken her place

maybe i was ready to leave you
or maybe i was just finished with the deceit
you decided i deserved

i could have loved you longer
if the promises you made
didn't slip through my fingers like sand

that
was the hard part
trying to fabricate a future out of fragments
trying to feel safe when all i saw was danger

maybe i was ready to leave you

or maybe you weren't ready for me to stay

- things i'm understanding

you need to speak up
and if anyone tries to make you think your story
does not hold the power
to change the end of someone else's
its because they don't know how to give up control

more people escape abuse
when we label it
and understand it
and when we
 refuse
 to accept it

anyone trying to silence your voice
is encouraging abuse
or worse

they're abusive

let your voice be hell on their ears

- things you need to remember

you have to tell yourself you'll get through it
every time you think of what the future might hold
you have to know you will survive

we say "i won't survive" so often we forget the power
of those words, because we forget it doesn't take long
to believe them

you have to tell yourself
every time doubt crowds your mind
every time you wonder how you could possibly go on
every time you are tired of being a warrior
in a world always at war
tell yourself that you will survive

tell yourself you are overrun with bravery and
resiliency and that you will not break despite the
weight the world gives you to carry

you have to tell yourself you'll get through it
because you have to believe it
to know it

so you can be a survivor
in a world of victims

and you wrestled with all these enormous things,
heavy things

things that threatened to shred your skin and bury
you alive
yet
    to
       all
          those
               around you

   invisible things

but
real things
and difficult things
don't you dare diminish that

don't for a second take away your right to be proud
of surviving the things you never talked about
that people never saw

 you are a warrior

there is magic in your bones

i sat with my grief a while today and let myself feel it's
presence. the heaviness in my chest and the ache of my
bones, the cry of my broken heart

i breathed in the sadness and felt it fill my hollow chest
with misery and regret until my cheeks burned red
and then

        i exhaled
the anger
the confusion
and my need to understand

and in the letting go, and the coming to terms
my grief
intertwined
with my joy and my peace
and my laughter made friends with the tears

you see i've learned, that grief
is walking with pain
and feeling the good

 despite

grief asked of me more than i had
my breath and my patience
my fight
my strength

and in the giving up i saw
just how much i had
so this one's for you:
to the world's best dad

and then, i understood
my life was not a story to be read
but a book to be written
i looked out at the rest of my life and for the first time,
i saw with fresh eyes
 a blank canvas

an opportunity to create a masterpiece out of me and
to let myself be who i knew i was
it was terrifying, and exhilarating
and the thought of all i could do overwhelmed me
but intertwined in the symphony,

        peace

as the future opened up, the standards fell away

i no longer wished to base my story on a series that
carried on far too long
i no longer wanted to play the games keeping everyone
cyclical

i want to break the cycle

and then, i felt it

the powerful rise of the captives
from generations before me
as we joined hands across dimensions and said,

"it is time to unleash
                    all
                         of me"

beginning does not have boundaries
this minute, the next

you can begin again
           and again

           and again

you are not a prisoner of the past
know this

and there it was

the slow return of softness
the laying down of weapons
the shedding of the armour

how strange
how foreign

how vulnerable

let the light shine into the darkest places
open me up and let me

drown
in
your
love

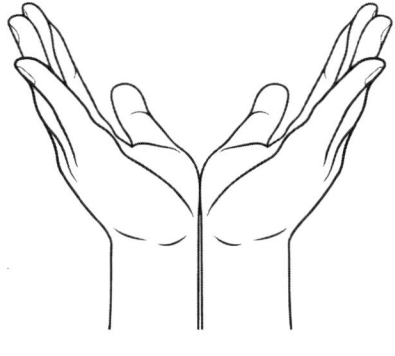

<u>giving in</u>

it wasn't time to start over
it was time to let go
to surrender
to everything had been avoiding

sometimes, i am a hurricane
destructive and reckless
but sometimes , a gentle rain
calm , still and quiet
i will need you to love me when the winds are strong
and the storm wreaks havoc
and tears fall like steady rain

i am a paradox
pulling you close one minute and pushing you away the
next
i fear suffocation
and abandonment in the same breath
 i will need you to love me when i reach for you
 and love me when i don't

i can be
         d e t a c h e d

cold, bitter, difficult
and passionate
full of light and joy

i need your love on the days i don't return it and
patience on the days i give too much

i will be warm
laughter in my eyes and sweetness on my lips
slipping sometimes into the grey of a stormy sky
my bones aching under the weight of heartbreak

love me on the days i am the sun
and harder when my skin is soaked in rain

i may love you with caution
                or a wild reckless spirit

i'll expect you to hurt me
                and pray that you don't

i don't need you
but i want you

so please
love me well

-- to the next one that loves me

<u>one</u>
it's april and you're far too drunk before you leave the
house, but you don't say no when he buys you tequila.
his eyes are the colour of clear blue skies and as hard as
you try to ignore the butterflies you can't help but
smile because something about him is different.

<u>two</u>
snow covers the city and your shoulders are tense- it
would be easier to never see him again and pretend all
the awful things you said you didn't, but he seems
eager, so something in you weakens, and although you
won't admit it- part of you has hope again.

<u>three</u>
when he tells you he loves you in may, you laugh,
because you think you know better and you think he's
not serious; but the sincerity in his eyes makes you
wonder if the things you learned to stay alive might be
worth leaving behind

<u>four</u>

the safety you feel in his arms on that gravel road was
bittersweet. to be loved with "i've got your back" and
the warmth of his heart during a panic attack is
overwhelming. your heart will break for the times you
willingly accepted less.

<u>five</u>

his skin glows in the june sun and you find yourself
coming to a sobering realization, he will either be the
most painful heartbreak, or the love of your life.

it was like i had been waiting for my life to start-
and then there he was

fucking living

not waiting for a single person to give him permission

i spent so much time
telling my secrets to the silence
that the sound of my voice
falling on your ears
was deafening

it felt unnatural hearing the thoughts in my head
brought to life
and i frantically searched your eyes for a sign
that some part of you

wasn't petrified

 by everything i've been hiding

- vulnerable

he taught me to bite my tongue every time he got angry with me for talking too much, and i'm sorry that leaves me speechless so frequently when there's so many things i want to tell you

"don't talk about them" he told me; frustrated by every reminder of anyone i was with before him. he made me feel dirty and used but i excused his behaviour because i hoped it would end, but with every apology that never came and all the things that didn't change i grew more desperate to fix the problems he pointed out in me

the things i could change that would make him stop yelling and telling me what to do, the ways i could shrink so he could feel bigger, the things i could carry so he would feel better

with every day that passed i learned to turn it off, i learned to exist within the lines and to put his needs before mine, i learned to pick myself apart and only see my flaws

so when he told me i was crazy
i think i started believing it

and i'm sorry that makes me withdraw

you see i'm still unlearning all the things he taught me,
i'm still untangling the indoctrination from the pieces
of me it overtook and i'm not sure how to tell you that
some of who i am is just what happened to me. i'm not
sure how to tell you that you remind me of who i was
before it became so hard for me to let you in

and i'm trying so hard to figure out if you are just a
chapter or the whole damn book

because i've never known how to not know what the
future holds because the unknown has always left me
broken and bleeding

he taught me that some people just take what they
want and will treat you like a possession
while they lie and say they love you

with you I'm learning love can be felt sooner than it's
said

- contrast

i could feel his heartbeat against my back as the
warmth of his breath trickled down my neck
and i wondered if he could feel mine beating too
giving away the words unsaid in the silence
we were unprepared for what we hoped for
and my mind raced in the anticipation of goodbye

but when he kissed me i swear

he tasted like fresh air

and i knew i was done

                  done searching
                  done pretending
and i hoped
                  done hurting

i guess more than anything i'm scared
of giving myself to another temporary person

i feel like everything in my life has been built
on a flimsy foundation of fiction

like all the happiness i've ever had is a mirage
a blur in the distance
that will always be just out of reach

and i'm so scared
of being vulnerable with someone
only to spend my life chasing the same in return

- the reasons i'm afraid

they say always leave them wanting more, but oh
it's impossible
 when it's always me that leaves
 wishing every second after i walk through your door
that i was back in your arms

i'm no good half measures
 or grey areas

my life is seesaw between all or nothing
and i'm always scared of being too much or just not
enough
do you see how fast i'm falling?

despite the way my knees get weak around you
and how alive you make me feel
i'm scared of trusting anyone to hold such power
and not abuse it

all i'm used to is excuses

i tried to figure out what it was
that was standing in the way

the final piece of my armour i wasn't ready to remove
the final wall i couldn't yet demolish
the chains that still existed on the piece of my heart
that desperately wanted to throw caution to the wind
and love you

with every fibre of my being

or maybe it's because, for once
i'm not scared that taking my time means wasting it
that if i'm too slow to love you
i might never have the chance

i guess what i'm trying to say is that you're the first
piece of hope
that hasn't felt temporary in a while

so be patient

i'm trying to love you like we have time

this was the year of houses; of boxes and packing and
bottles of wine
this was the year of early mornings, late nights, and the
year of smoke filled lungs

it was the year of feeling hopeless
building walls

and the year of isolation

this was the year of trying too hard
and the year of 'never enough'.

and, this was the year

of

Him

and the voice called out, asking if i was ready
to step through the open door and lay my wandering
soul to rest

but for once it didn't ask me
to leave
        myself
                behind

"you are home"
it said
"and it's time to unpack"

i could feel this stirring inside of me as the voice became
my own

i am home
i think i've been here the whole time

and i am no longer
alone

you've carried so many heavy things
such a long way

it's time to leave them behind

maybe we just start here
forget the past and love each other with a clean slate

maybe we could love each other
as if we were not broken
and scared
and as if the world never blackened our hearts
and taught us to be afraid of the very thing we want
most

- i think i'm ready to fall in love

you are clarity and silence
amidst confusion and noise
you are strong, steady, and calm
spinning beautiful words
slowly quieting my chaotic thoughts

"it would be easy to love you"
i thought

it had all seem too complicated before
too difficult and messy
forced

but you were simple
a beautiful sunrise
after a long, dark night

and then there was light

the night we met nervous fireworks jolted through our
bodies and every time you kissed me i felt a little more
alive

the oceans in your eyes dared to drown me as our
bodies sighed in harmony
your breath and mine a symphony in the silence of the
hazy summer night

God, our love is a wildfire
burning hotter with every minute i spend in your arms
threatening to consume me while i try to hang on to
common sense, my body spent
overwhelmed not only by all you are but all you are not

i think i might be lost in the wilderness of us
somewhere down a road that seems infinite
and i'm sinking in the quicksand
shaken to the core
the sound of distant war muddled
by a sweet familiarity
and the fear of the unknown

one day you're wondering if the earth might
crumble beneath you and the next your
desperately praying it doesn't

- Him

today he said i love you across the kitchen completely
sober and i was a little taken off guard
but
    my God

it felt good

i think this is what love is supposed to feel like
simple
electric
romantic

he's exactly what i dreamed of and more

i did not fall
in love
      with
           you

i barely noticed when it happened

it was not
abrupt
    or
       loud

it was
      soft
        and
            familiar

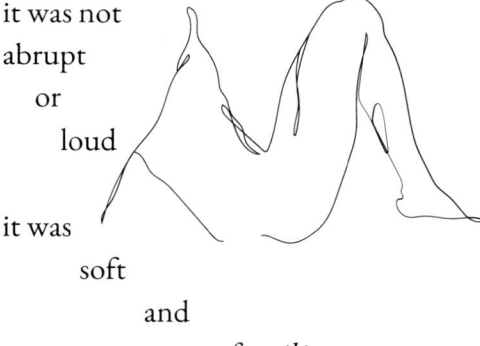

today i am closer to knowing myself than ever
before and the strange thing is that in the most
contradictory sense

i have absolutely no idea who i am

i have never existed in a space where the galaxies in
the sky outshone those in my head

i fought for years to find reality, stability
building walls out of facts
weapons for the chaos

but at some point i began to realize
that although there is comfort in knowledge
and truth

i am no God
not meant to know it all

but
what i do know is that you are the first person
who's gaze held mine
despite the monsters in my eyes

and i know that when you laugh
i mean
really laugh

a glimpse of something magical
flickers in your smile

and
best of all
i know that your arms
feel like the eye of the hurricane

and i know
that
is home

- the important things

he,
is a stunning mystery
an overwhelming thing to love.

i am
in
awe

of the masterpiece of us

of the crippling inability my pen has accepted
to string letters together in anything less than
shallow attempts

i feel for him
so
ferociously
that he strips me of my essence
and lays my bones bare

he is the first thing
i have found
which cannot be defined
nor
picked apart

the epitome of all
that is
good

so i will wring out my heart
spilling blood to blank pages

i will strive to capture
the profound
and the iridescent
intricacies

of
all that he is

**what an honour to aspire
to such an impossible task**

i love him in a language i do not understand, in words my lips lack the courage to speak. i love him in the stolen seconds. the moments after hitting snooze where the soft morning light spills over his skin

i love him in the vibrance of his laughter, how it leaps from his chest and slows me to a crawl

loving him is letting go, of all assumptions, all fears
breaking free of the demons that built up my walls
and loving him is giving in
it is overwhelming and terrifying and thrilling
how his eyes rip me open and leave me exposed
stripped of pride and the comfort of seclusion

and loving him is simple
it is the steadiness of his breath as his fingers trace maps on my skin
it is the closeness and the comfort
his body folding into mine until i do not know where he ends
and i begin

you told me you loved me one night after i had known you only a month. i thought it was cute how you said it; i couldn't be mad that you were drunk because it didn't sound sloppy or insincere, it sounded like the beginning of a story.

i told you i loved you a month after that, after biting my tongue out of fear wondering if you were really all you appeared to be but when you hugged me and told me i didn't have to face my pain alone, i knew that even if this wasn't forever, i did love you.

i love you like a best friend, someone i respect. someone who has shown me loyalty and kindness when i am at my lowest, and has made me feel more accepted than anyone in my life before. i love your integrity, honest, and the way you make me laugh.

and although it may not mean the same thing as it means if we're still saying it 5 years from now, i love you.

- time capsule

his smile warms my body from the inside out. he knows that my favorite chips are all dressed and when i say 'two scoops' i really mean three. he slow dances in the kitchen with me while drinking tequila and we're both silly drunk laughing so hard we cry

he tells me i'm beautiful. he says it when the morning light falls upon my face and most importantly i believe him. on the days my eyes are sad he buys me flowers and tells me he's got my back; and i cry in front of him, i think that means i trust him

when he asks me if i've eaten today and i tell him i've had breakfast he knows i don't eat breakfast and makes me eggs and toast.

he kissed me good morning, goodnight, and just because, and he always has the exact right words to say when i'm overthinking things.

he likes his coffee black and his beer cold, he's got a good heart and kind eyes and he calls his mom more than once a week

i've frustrated the hell out of him more than once, but despite my fears we came through it okay when he told me he loved me the first time i laughed. he's not afraid of heights which means he didn't fall in fearful and immature love with me. he jumped in, eyes wide open

now when he tells me he loves me, i tell him i love him too because despite my fear of heights falling isn't scary with him

i love him

and there is no reason to say 'more than' because i know now that i've never known love before

so when i tell you to wait for the kind of love that doesn't take, a love void of fear and understanding of mistakes, i mean it

wait for the guy who makes you feel safe in every single way, and gives you a hug when you've had a bad day and says 'everything will be okay'

wait for the one who's been waiting for you

there is freedom in the understanding
that you are only half

a conversation
an argument
a solution
a relationship

the responsibility was never all yours

i thought love was like a garden
growing with time and attention
a thing to take care of

but with you, love is like a flame
ignited inside us with sparks
an inferno in seconds

you taught me
 love
 had never been
    seperate

i thought love was like a garden
and maybe it was with those before
but though they are alive, it's only for a while
gardens die
and do not survive a storm

i thought love was like a garden
but with you it is a force within
a purifying flame
destroying our sin

-

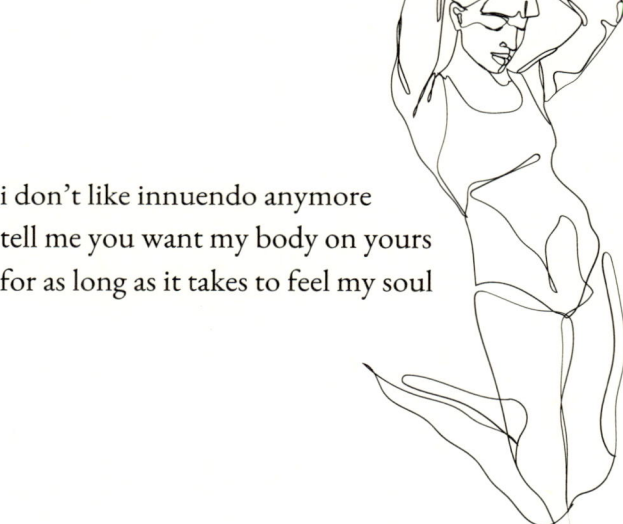

i don't like innuendo anymore
tell me you want my body on yours
for as long as it takes to feel my soul

and in the silence of 2 a.m.
we made love
and art

i want you to kiss me so hard
that i forget how to breathe
and my legs go weak

put your hands on my pale skin
and teach me a language in which we don't speak
devour me
 my love

i am yours alone

your arms will always feel the most
like home

i felt the flames lick
and engulf
you
      and
          i

our veins glowing
and the air thick with smoke

and in the presence of you
it was there
i was
consumed

kiss me in the chaos of a late august storm
press your body into mine
and let your lips steal my words

there
right there

as the rain soaks our bones
and thunder shakes our souls
kiss me so i know you can handle the storm

like the soft glow of june sun
or the smell of coffee at 6 a.m.
like the inescapable feeling of awe that soaks through
your skin as you stand atop a mountain

like city lights
and
every night you stayed awake to see the stars

- favorites

his eyes held my gaze for much longer
than i ever held his hand
infinite hues with faint flecks of gold
stars illuminating the ebony sky
fierce, but kind

i wanted to let him read my story
but the pages were worn and dog eared
stained with tears and dirt
they were not full of eloquent words
or inspiring stories
they were full of scars and monsters

but as his eyes met mine
and my heartbeat hastened
racing a thousand miles per second

i remembered that sometimes people are safe

so i softened

allowing his strong hands to peruse through my pages
his forehead furrowed in deep thought
as each word
each story
seeped into his mind
soaking into the corners
and bleeding out into his thoughts

and as he finished,
he smiled
and i noticed a few less crinkles
 a few less stains

for once someone read the story
instead of burning the book

the most selfless gift he gave me
was his lack of expectations

- he loves me as i am

and learning to love you started
with learning to love myself

none of it was poetic, when it was all said and done
it was not a story, but a catastrophe

chaos, in all its glory

but that
is the best part-
you made it poetic

because
you
are the magic

you were always the magic

do you see it now?
look at the masterpiece, look at the majesty
the very fact that you are standing here today makes
the devil run in fear
do you not see the bravery in your mere existence?

you have walked through fire
you have fought your demons
you have faced your most painful truths and you have
sought out wisdom even when it brought loneliness
you have carried burdens for so long that we're not
your own

you are a phoenix
the definition of beauty from ashes
a light in the midst of a dark world despite how hard
the darkness tried to consume you

every day you wake up and fight
every day you wake up and battle insecurities and
worries and responsibilities that make you feel like you
are suffocating
you are human, in all your glory

it's time to stop hiding

you tell me to be quiet
as if you do not understand

thunder

      bows

          to

              no one

this year, my anger softened
the sharp edges of my heart melted
into vulnerability
and for the first time
the air didn't sting my lungs
my bones didn't break
under the weight of regret
and i finally sighed in relief

peace

after years of misery
of chaos and violence and losing my mind

peace

how marvellous to know it existed all along

when i was a little girl my dad told me faith could move
mountains
i waited for the day i'd pray and a mountain would
pick itself up and be cast into the sea,
but it didn't happen

as i got older i realized, faith does move mountains
 right in front of our eyes
every single day

but not in the way most people think

i realized recently i've had it all wrong
waiting for mountains to unearth and be turned on
their heads

the thing i didn't see and perhaps the key
is that mountains are moved in front of our eyes
 all the time
 over time

water flows from glaciers carrying rocks miles away
shaping peaks and valleys into the landscape
creating depth from a formless world

now i understand
moving mountains requires patience
diligence
 and unwavering faith

i pray i never forget the majesty of the mountains
that once didn't exist
when my patience starts to wear thin
and i feel like my progress is slim

i always wanted to write about important things
and today as i sat on the couch watching sitcoms
in a cloud of nostalgia
i realized that every moment is important
because *God*, i wanted to die last year

i wanted to stop living and existing under the weight
of every mistake i'd made
and i never thought i'd catch myself smiling again

 but here i am

the happiest i've ever been
and i want to write about every damn second of my life
because it's a fucking miracle

i want to write about the ecstasy in every drop of sun
as it cascades over my skin
and the whimsy of every snowflake on my eyelashes
and the smell of hot chocolate coalesced
with the crackling of the fire

i want to write about the lazy days
and my best friends laugh
the sound of birds outside my window
and the cerulean sky

God, i never want to forget what it feel like to be
overwhelmingly alive

i always wanted to write about important things, so i
will write until i die

when i think of what a friend should be, i think of you
i think of the first time i realized i could cry in front of
you, and how you didn't look away or try to make it
better, you just

stayed

you looked at my broken pieces and saw someone to
believe in

even when i didn't believe in me too

you are so much more
than one thing you've done
or been
or said
a symphony is filled with many notes
and you
with many parts

i don't care what you do for a living
i don't care how much you weigh
or what the colour of your skin is

you see recently i realized
i've been giving out friendships to people
who can't even give me respect
so no

i don't care if the car you drive cost 100k
or what kind of watch you use to tell time
i just care that you're kind

hold space for the pieces of me that still need to heal
help me soften me rough edges and tell me i'm
intelligent
beautiful
capable

build me up instead of tearing me down because i
don't care what you do
or what you have
i just care who you are

i care that you take the time to understand me
and give me the benefit of the doubt
even when something i say is
maybe
borderline not okay

because i want people around me
who recognize i'm trying
and i'm dying to be understood

i don't care what you do

i care how i feel when i'm with you

a friendly reminder, because i think you might need it
that you are so much more than you know

you are more that the photographs you dislike
because "that's your bad side"
and you're more than the weight
you keep trying to hide

i wish you could see through my eyes
for a change
past the things that society claims are important
to the magic that lays dormant
waiting for the day you say "screw it"
and stop existing simply to please everyone else

a friendly reminder, because i need it too
that your worth is not made up of all the times you
messed up

your failures are not a tattoo, but a bruise

you see you are not defined by the times you fell down
or messed up

who you are in this world is not a number on a scale
or how often you're stressed
and feel like giving up
not at all

you are the softness you hold
despite the chaos you've survived

you are the forgiveness you choose
in the face of being alive
in a world that offers no reprieve
from hate so heavy it dares to make you believe
that rising is impossible

yet you continue to show that its probable

every time you stand up, and try again

- for when you don't see your worth

---

if it is the last thing you do
learn to love every
dark piece of you

---

the truth is
until we stop talking about our friends with mental
illness in a way that puts them down, or diminishes
their right to speak up for themselves, or to have
opinions, or to struggle

until we stop using mental illness as a reason to talk
about somebody behind their back or to make
assumptions about their life based on things we think
we know

and until we start treating mental illness like a broken
leg and sending get well soon cards to our friends
battling depression from their beds, and until we hold
their hand during a panic attack and lend a listening ear
when they need it

until we do these things, the stigma doesn't end
you see the stigma's only half we have to change the
way we act. we have to empathize, to understand that
our friends with mental illness are really just our friends
and they need us to show up for them

that's how the stigma ends

and tonight, i'm writing

sitting in the living room while he cooks dinner and the smell of fresh spices fills the air instead of tension and silence

i think this has to be the first time in a while i've felt alright and i'm miles away from the place that you left me but part of me feels guilty and probably not for reasons you think

i know you can't stop a ship from sinking but sometimes i wish that i could. sometimes i wish i had been strong enough not to break under the pressure of loving you when things were so far from okay, and some days i look around at this life i've arrived in and wonder if you'll get to feel this again

maybe
that's stupid, to care so much for someone that destroyed you
but that's all i know how to do

tonight, i'm writing
in a house with four walls that's filled with warmth
and i can't help but hoping that you'll find this too

as much as i hated you
i've come to forgive you

and part of that means understanding
that you did your best and i was a mess

neither of us destined for the future we expected
but i know now that's the way it should be

things work out the way they're supposed to

and at the end of the day
i know you'll be okay

- closure

and this, is my heart
in
your
hands

my journey
my story
my darkness
my light

'unpacking' is my story of survival
a time capsule of all the moments where i couldn't
contain the chaos inside
so i asked my pen for help
but more than that, it is the story of how i found
myself

i pray you find pieces of yourself in these words too

- about

Made in United States
North Haven, CT
05 February 2022

15726785R00119